In the Home

JON RICHARDS

Chrysalis Children's Books

First published in the UK in 2004 by
Chrysalis Children's Books
An imprint of Chrysalis Books Group Plc
The Chrysalis Building, Bramley Road,
London W10 6SP

ISBN 1 84458 111 X

British Library Cataloguing in Publication Data for this
book is available from the British Library.

Editorial Manager *Joyce Bentley*
Editorial Assistant *Camilla Lloyd*
Produced by Tall Tree Ltd
Designer *Ed Simkins*
Editor *Kate Simkins*
Consultant *Jon Kirkwood*
Picture Researcher *Lorna Ainger*

Printed in China

Some of the more unfamiliar words used in this book
are explained in the glossary on page 31.

Typography *Natascha Frensch*
Read Regular, READ SMALLCAPS and Read Space;
European Community Design Registration 2003 and
Copyright © Natascha Frensch 2001-2004
Read Medium, Read Black and *Read Slanted*
Copyright © Natascha Frensch 2003-2004

READ™ is a revolutionary new typeface that will enchance
children's understanding through clear, easily recognisable
character shapes. With its evenly spaced and carefully
designed characters, READ™ will help children at all stages
to improve their literacy skills, and is ideal for young readers,
reluctant readers and especially children with dyslexia.

Photo Credits
The publishers would like to thank the following for their kind permission
to reproduce the photographs:
Lorna Ainger: 21b, 23b, 28t, 29c AKG Images: Bibliotheque Nationale, Paris
Alamy.com: Ginsberg 4, Martine Hamilton Knight/Arcaid 7t, Robert Harding
World Imagery 14, Justin Kase 5b, 28bl Art Archive: Bibliotheque des Arts
Decoratifs, Paris/Dagli Orti 22 Courtesy Baxi Potterton/Baxi Heating UK
Ltd.: 9t Corbis: Bettmann 10, 25tr, FC br, William Gottlieb 21t, BC, Historical
Picture Archive 12, Michael Nicholson 24, Galen Rowell 6, 30, FC tl Digital
Vision: 7b Courtesy Dolphin Bathrooms: 2, 23t, FC c Courtesy Electrolux
(Timeline): 1, 15b, 17b Getty: Hulton Archive 13b, 18, 19cl, 20, 29bl, MPI 11t,
David Silverman 9, Yoshikazu Tsuno 25l, Adrian Ace Williams 15t Courtesy L
Electronics: 26, 27t, 29tr, FC bl Robert Opie: 16 OSRAM Limited: 19r, 31 R
Features Ltd.: Voisin/Phanie 13t Science Photo Library: Alex Bartel 5t Still
Pictures: Martin Bond 27b Tall Tree Ltd.: 11b, 17t, 29br, FC tr

Contents

Building methods

The need for shelter is one of our most basic requirements. Since people first started to build their own homes around 12 000 BC, the materials and methods used to construct our homes have changed greatly.

The earliest homes were either natural shelters or tents. However, as people started to settle in one place, more permanent homes, made from stronger materials, such as wood, mud or stone, were needed.

▼ Many medieval homes, such as this one, were built with a visible wooden framework, which was filled in with mud and dung.

◀ Today, concrete is poured around thick bars of iron or steel to make a structure that is strong. This is called reinforced concrete.

EUREKA!

In about 4000 BC, the people of Ancient Mesopotamia made the first oven-dried bricks. They mixed mud with clay and baked the bricks hard inside a special fire, called a kiln. Bricks are still a commonly used building material.

The Romans started to use concrete to make buildings around 200 BC, and they were also the first people to use clear glass in their homes to let in light. Today, many modern materials are used to construct homes, including plastic and fibreglass.

All shapes and sizes

As the range of materials used in house construction has increased and the needs of people have changed, so the size and shape of the homes we live in has altered. This has created a great variety of homes around the world.

In the ancient world, particularly in poorer homes or colder climates, families lived, ate and slept in single-room buildings. Houses with many rooms, such as Roman villas, were for the wealthy or for those living in hot countries where they didn't need to huddle together to keep warm.

▼ The earliest people were nomads. They carried their homes, usually tents, with them. Today, some nomads, such as these people in China, live in modern as well as traditional tents.

◀ Modern Western houses are usually built with more than one storey and many rooms for different purposes, such as sleeping, eating and bathing.

Today, homes vary from simple huts to large mansions with many rooms. The type of home people choose depends on where they live, the number of people living there and the climate. The cost and the availability of building materials are also important.

EUREKA!

The invention of the safety lift in 1853 by Elisha Otis was an important step in building development. It provided a safe way of climbing many storeys quickly and was one of the main reasons that very tall buildings, such as skyscrapers, became possible.

Keeping warm

Humans started to use fire to keep warm nearly 1.5 million years ago. Open fires remained the main way to heat homes until the 19th century, when central heating became popular.

In the earliest buildings, an open fire was positioned in the middle of a room and people gathered around it to stay warm. Smoke would leave through a hole in the middle of the roof.

◄ Chimneys were first built into homes in medieval Europe. The smoke from the fireplace travelled up a flue, or channel, in the wall. It then exited the building via a chimney stack on the roof.

In the 19th century, the need to heat large factories led to the development of central heating. Today, the most common types of central heating use either warm air or hot water. Warm air is released from ducts into the house. Hot water travels in pipes to metal radiators that then give off heat.

◄ The air or water in a central-heating system is heated by burning fuel, such as gas. Most European homes have water heaters called boilers.

EUREKA!

One of the earliest forms of central heating was developed by the Romans. Known as a hypocaust, it used fire to warm the air. The hot air flowed through spaces beneath the floor, heating the rooms above. The remains of a hypocaust are shown here.

Cooking at home

People have been cooking food for thousands of years to make it safe to eat and taste better. Many cooking methods have been developed from the open fire to electric ovens.

The earliest forms of cooking involved heating the food over an open fire. Around 2000 BC, the Ancient Egyptians became the first people to bake food, such as bread, in clay ovens.

◀ Fires were used to cook food by our ancestors many thousands of years ago.

The first cooking ranges were introduced in the 1780s. They were made up of an open fire with an oven and hobs on either side. The first electric oven was installed in a hotel in 1889. Most modern ovens are heated by electricity or gas. Some contain fans that circulate the hot air to make the food cook more quickly and evenly.

▲ Cooking ranges, such as this one from the 19th century, included hobs on which pots and pans were placed to boil or fry food and ovens in which food was roasted or baked.

LOOK CLOSER

The microwave oven was invented by Percy Spencer in 1946. It works by producing a high-energy field that causes tiny molecules inside food to vibrate. This vibration creates the heat that cooks the food. Microwave ovens cook food in less time than ordinary ovens.

Keeping food

For thousands of years, people have been preserving food to make it last longer. This meant that food could be stored in the home for future use. Today, most modern homes have refrigerators or freezers to keep food fresh.

▲ Food, such as fish or meat, was hung in a smoke house, where smoke from a fire was used to preserve the food.

The Sumerians, whose civilisation flourished around 3000 BC, were the first people to dry and smoke fish to preserve it. Another early storage method, called pickling, used a salty liquid or vinegar to preserve food.

◀ In a refrigerator, food can be kept fresh for a long time. This means people do not have to buy new produce every day.

Around 1000 BC, the Chinese were one of the first people to keep food fresh by keeping it in snow stored in their cellars. Ice was used in cool boxes and ice houses to keep food fresh until the middle of the 19th century. Then, in 1834, American Jacob Perkins invented the refrigerator.

EUREKA!

After spending time in Canada as a fur trader, Clarence Birdseye noticed how local people there froze food in the ice to preserve it. He brought this technique back with him to the USA. In 1929, he introduced the first freezer and started to sell frozen foods.

Washing clothes

Keeping clothes clean has always required a lot of effort. The development of washing machines in the 1800s meant that what once took all day could now be done in a few hours.

The earliest records of cleaning clothes dates back to Ancient Egypt around 3500 BC. From then until the 19th century, the method of washing clothes changed very little, relying largely on pounding and scrubbing clothes by hand to clean them.

▼ Traditional methods of cleaning clothes are still used in many parts of the world today.

The first soap powder was introduced in 1843. Before then people had used clay, animal fat and even urine to help clean clothes. Many machines have been invented to make the hard work of doing the laundry easier. They include the washing machine and, in 1909, the tumble drier.

◄ Early washing devices included the washboard. The ridges meant that clothes could be thoroughly scrubbed.

EUREKA!

In 1851, James King invented a hand-operated washing machine with a spinning drum that pounded the clothes together to remove dirt. The first electric washing machine, designed by Alva Fisher in 1907, also had a drum, as do most modern machines.

House cleaning

The invention of vacuum cleaners revolutionised house work. They replaced traditional methods of cleaning, such as beating and sweeping, which were tiring and messy, and they made it quicker and easier to get rid of dirt.

Many different tools have been used to clean homes over the years, including beaters, brushes, brooms and feather dusters. Little changed in the design of house-cleaning tools until the start of the 20th century.

The DOOM of the DUSTER the BRUSH and the BROOM

THE ASPIRATOR

CLEANS EVERYTHING BY AIR SUCTION

◄ This early, hand-operated vacuum cleaner sucked up dirt, but it was heavy and awkward to move around.

LOOK CLOSER

Some modern vacuum cleaners do not need to use bags to collect dust. Instead, air and dust are sucked up from the floor and spun very quickly. This spinning flings any dust to one side where it is collected in a plastic cylinder which can be emptied when full and used again.

▼ Modern vacuum cleaners are designed to be light and easy to use. Many have disposable bags to collect the dust.

In 1901, Hubert Booth showed that you could suck dirt out of a seat and into a handkerchief. He went on to invent the vacuum cleaner. Portable vacuum cleaners were developed by William Henry Hoover in 1926. They used brushes to beat the carpet and an electric pump to suck the dirt up into a bag.

Light in the home

The development of lighting in the home meant that people were able to carry out activities that previously could only be done during the day.

The earliest lights were simple oil lamps made by cave dwellers from hollowed out stones around 40 000 BC. Other early forms of light included burning torches or candles. Although dim by modern standards, these early lights still allowed people to work and play after the sun had set.

▼ Oil lamps, such as this one from the 18th century, could produce enough light to read a book by.

EUREKA!

In trying to invent the world's first light bulb, Thomas Edison tried many different materials, including platinum and human hair. The problem was in finding a filament that could glow without burning out. In the summer of 1880, Edison discovered that fibres of carbonised bamboo made the best filaments for a bulb.

OSRAM DULUX EL
20W/41-827 · 220-240V
50/60Hz · Made in Germany

n the 18th century, homes began to be lit with gas, roviding a constant and reliable source of light. he gas, usually coal gas, was piped into homes nd burned in lamps. With the invention of the ght bulb, gas was replaced by electricity, allowing eople to light a dark room at the flick of a switch.

▲ Many modern light bulbs are designed to last a long time and to be energy efficient.

Entertainment

Amusements in the home have changed over the years, from story-telling and playing music to radio, television and, more recently, computer games.

Traditional forms of household entertainment were usually performed by family members who would sing songs and play games. The first entertainment machine appeared in 1877 when Thomas Edison invented the phonograph, an early type of record player.

◄ Victorian families would often gather in the parlour to listen to music.

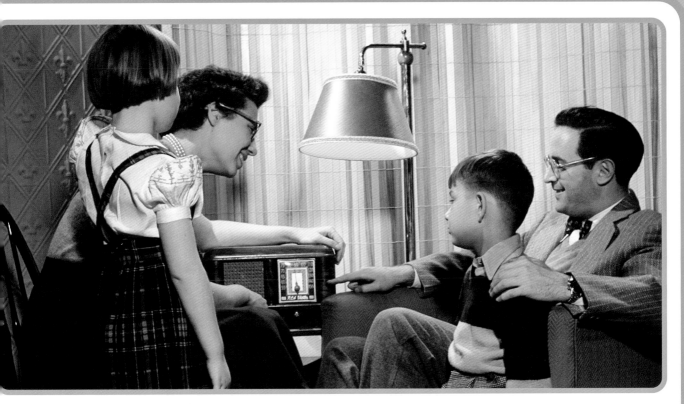

The first radio signal was transmitted in 1895 by Italian Guglielmo Marconi, but it was not until 1920 that regular radio broadcasts started. Small portable radios for the home appeared soon after. Then, in 1928, the first regular television service started, beaming pictures into people's homes for the first time.

▲ Radio and, later, television brought entertainment, news and information from the studio or theatre into a family's living room.

LOOK CLOSER

Since John Logie Baird invented the television in 1924, it has become a central feature in many homes around the world. In 2001, there were 248 million television sets in the US alone, with 98.2 per cent of households owning at least one. The average number of TVs was 2.4 per household.

In the bathroom

Since ancient times, people have bathed or showered to clean themselves. Regular bathing, however, was only possible for the rich. The introduction of plumbing into homes in the 20th century meant that ordinary people were able to wash daily.

Ancient peoples placed great importance on staying clean, although often it was only the rich who could afford to do so. Ruins from Ancient Egypt, Greece and Rome include special public bathrooms, bathhouses and pools.

◄ A visit to a Roman bathhouse involved steaming, cleaning and massaging the body. Famous Roman baths include the baths at Caracalla in Rome.

Private bathrooms did not become popular until the development of plumbing and cheap fuel to heat the water. Before then, washing was done in wooden or metal tubs with water heated on a fire.

▲ Modern homes often have an indoor bathroom with a bath and shower combined.

EUREKA!

Soap was developed around 500 BC. The Phoenicians used a mixture of goat's fat and wood ashes to clean themselves. The Celts of Britain also used a mixture of animal fat and plant ashes, calling it saipo, from which the modern name comes.

Toilets

One problem with having so many homes close together was what to do with the human waste that was created. If it's not removed safely, sewage becomes a foul-smelling problem that can cause disease.

The earliest toilets discovered belonged to the Indus civilisation of Asia. They had simple brick lavatories with seats that opened into a cesspit or drain. Although many civilisations built toilets, the main problem was developing a sewage system to get rid of the waste.

▼ The Romans built public toilets with holes carved into stone seats, such as these from Ephesus in Turkey, which was part of the Roman Empire.

EUREKA!

Important dates marking the development of the toilet include: 1596, Sir John Harrington published a design for a flushing toilet; 1775, Alexander Cummings patented the S-shaped bend to trap bad smells; and 1884, Thomas Crapper's valveless cistern meant toilets could flush efficiently.

▲ This ultra-modern toilet from Japan contains a seat warmer and an air freshener.

Without a system of carrying sewage away safely, diseases, such as cholera and typhoid, were common. It was not until the 19th century that people understood the connection between sewage and disease and started to build systems that could carry waste away.

The future home

With all the modern devices in our homes today, how can things possibly improve? Well, inventors are looking at ways of making the places we live in even easier to look after and kinder to the environment.

The development of the computer in the 20th century led to the creation of machines that can carry out boring tasks, such as cleaning. With more parents at work, this means people can spend less time on household chores and more time relaxing.

◄ This refrigerator is linked to the Internet and can order food automatically from suppliers when stocks run low.

One of the latest developments has been the introduction of the Internet into homes. Electrical systems in a home will be connected to the Internet and controlled via any online computer. This means that people will be able to turn on lights, heating or the oven before they return home!

▲ The latest vacuum cleaners are robots. The machines contain computers that guide them around a room, cleaning it entirely on their own.

LOOK CLOSER

Heating and lighting our homes is expensive and causes pollution. New, cleaner ways of supplying energy are being tried. These include solar power, which uses special panels to change the sun's rays into electricity. Solar energy doesn't pollute the atmosphere.

Timeline

• C.12 000 BC. The first homes are built.

• C.8000 BC. The first towns and cities are established.

• C.500 BC. The Phoenicians develop the first soap.

• AD 216. The Romans complete the building of the Baths of Caracalla in Rome.

• C.2000 BC. The Ancient Egyptians use clay ovens to bake food.

• C.1780. The first cooking ranges are introduced.

12 000 BC

• C.1000 BC. The Chinese use snow to keep food cold in cellars.

• 1834. Jacob Perki invents the refrigerator.

• C.3000 BC. Earliest evidence of candles from Ancient Egyptian candlesticks.

• C.200 BC. The Romans use concrete to construct buildings.

• 1843. The first soap powder for clothes is introduced.

• C.3000 BC. The Ancient Sumerians dry and smoke their food to preserve it.

• 1775. Alexander Cummings patents S-bend in toilets.

• 1596. Sir John Harrington designs the first flushing toilet.

• C.4000 BC. Bricks are invented in Mesopotamia.

• 1851. James King develops the first washing machine with a spinning drum.

• 1853. Elisha Otis develops the safety lift.

• 1884. Thomas Crapper develops the valveless water cistern.

• 1907. Alva Fisher designs the first electric washing machine.

• 1909. The first electric tumble driers are introduced.

• 1920. The world's first commercial radio station starts broadcasting.

• 1924. John Logie Baird invents the television.

• 1926. William Henry Hoover creates the first practical household vacuum cleaner.

• 2003. Robot vacuum cleaners are available for the first time.

TODAY

• 1901. Hubert Booth demonstrates how vacuum cleaning could work.

• 1895. The first radio signal is transmitted by Guglielmo Marconi.

• 1946. Percy Spencer invents the microwave oven.

• c.1970. The first home video games are sold.

• 1929. Clarence Birdseye sells frozen food.

• 1880. Thomas Edison develops a working light bulb.

Factfile

• Concrete was invented by the Romans, who mixed volcanic ash with water, lime and stone fragments to form a rock-like material when hard.

• The largest home that is not a palace is St Emmeram Castle in Regensburg, Germany. It has 517 rooms.

• The Roman Baths of Caracalla in Rome were some of the largest baths built in the empire. They could hold up to 1600 bathers at one time.

• The tallest residential building in the world is the Trump Tower in New York City, USA, with 72 storeys.

• The average adult spends nearly 1670 hours watching the television each year – that's the equivalent of 70 whole days!

• Candles are some of the earliest inventions known. This has been shown by the discovery of candlesticks from Ancient Crete and Egypt that date back to 3000 BC.

Glossary

Boiler
A machine that heats water. The hot water is then pumped through pipes and radiators around a home as part of a central heating system.

Cistern
A tank for storing water. A small cistern is connected to a toilet to store the water used for flushing.

Concrete
A building material made out of cement, sand, stone and water that can be poured when it is wet and dries to form a hard material.

Filament
A coil of wire that is found at the centre of a light bulb. It glows brightly when an electrical current flows through it.

Indus civilisation
A civilisation that flourished about 4000 years ago in what is now modern Pakistan.

Mesopotamia
A region of the Middle East situated in what is now modern Iraq that was the site of several ancient civilisations.

Nomad
A person who moves about from place to place in search of food and water.

Patent
This is official recognition that an inventor is the only person who can make, use and sell a device.

Phoenicians
An ancient culture that existed about 3000 years ago in what is now the countries of Lebanon, Syria and Israel.

Plumbing
A network of pipes that circulate water around the house.

Preserve
To stop food rotting by using methods such as freezing.

Sewage
Waste matter from homes and factories that is carried away in sewers and drains to water treatment plants. There it is cleaned before being released into streams and rivers.

Sumer
An ancient culture that flourished about 6500 years ago in modern Iraq.

OSRAM DULUX EL
20W/41-827 · 220-240V
50/60Hz · Made in Germany

Index